ISBN - 978-0-9917887-7-4

This book is dedicated with love to all children everywhere around the world.
Much gratitude and special thanks to Angel Brkic whose artistic talent has brought our beloved characters to life.

Matlox Publishing

"It is going to be a good day today," Lizzy said as she sat down to eat her breakfast.

"You seem happy this morning," her mother said. "Oh I am," said Lizzy. "The teacher told us that a boy from China is going to be in our class and he doesn't speak any English, but I really want to be his friend," Lizzy said.

When Lizzy got to class, she sat next to the new boy whose name was Chin and she smiled at him and said, "Hi I am Lizzy."

Chin looked at Lizzy and turned away. He looked scared. Lizzy kept trying to talk to Chin, but the more she tried the sadder and more scared he looked.

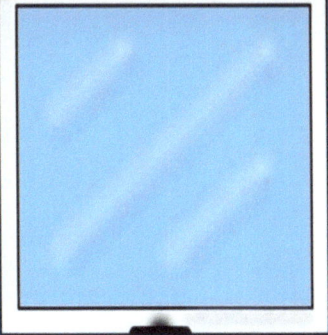

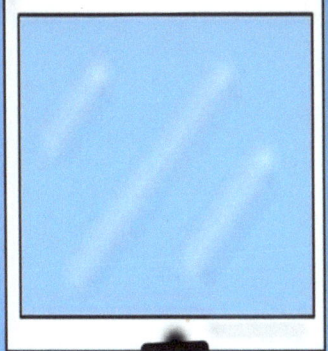

Chin even started to cry when the teacher asked him a question.

When Lizzy got home from school she went to her room and sat on her bed.

She closed her eyes and imagined what it would be like to be in a different country where everyone spoke a language that she didn't understand. Lizzy thought about how scared and alone she would feel if she was Chin.

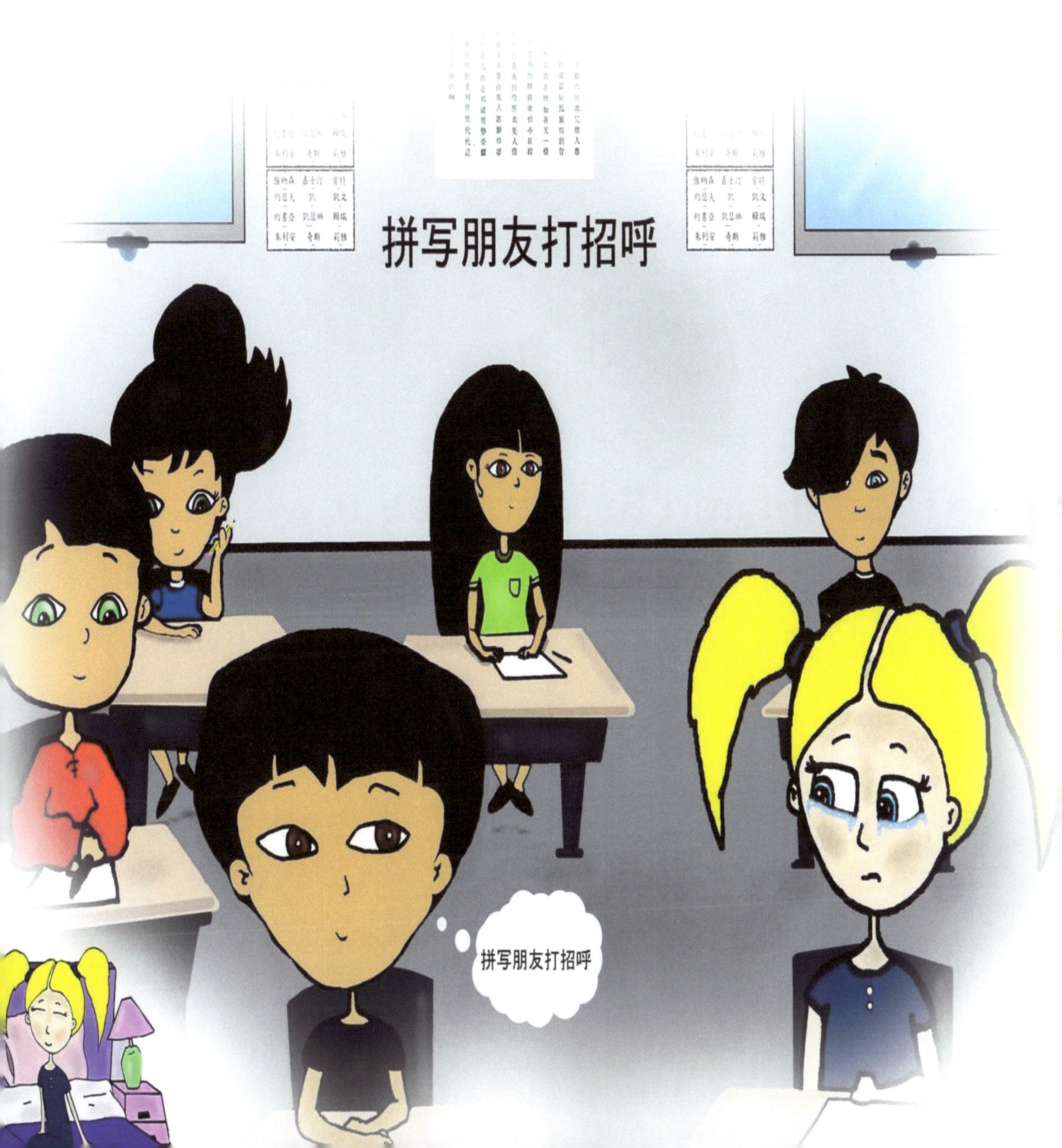

She thought and thought about what she could do to let Chin know she wanted to be his friend. Lizzy jumped off the bed.

She found some paper, coloured pencils and other supplies and then she began to cut and paste things on the paper.

When Lizzy had finished, she put the paper in her back pack so she would remember to take it to school in the morning.

When Lizzy got to class, she showed the paper to Chin. He looked at it, smiled and then he pointed to himself with a questioning look.

Lizzy nodded her head. "Yes it is you Chin" she said.

When the bell rang Lizzy walked over to Chin and took his hand. "Let's go play at my house."

"I want you to meet my friends, Tommy and Victoria," said Lizzy. They all skipped rope, bounced a ball, and played tag. Chin was laughing and having fun.

When Lizzy sat down for supper her mother asked, "How did you get Chin to understand that you wanted to play with him?"

Lizzy ran to the closet and pulled out the paper she had shown Chin. "This is what I did Momma," Lizzy said. "I put myself in Chin's place and I knew that I would feel scared and alone too if I didn't understand what people were saying. I thought I could talk to him with pictures."

"That was a great idea Lizzy," her mother said as she gave her a hug.
"Everyone understands the language of kindness."

www.ingramcontent.com/pod-product-compliance
Lightning Source LLC
Chambersburg PA
CBHW041550040426
42447CB00002B/127